I0837962

Let's Learn Funny ABC

ABC

Apple

Banana

Coconut

Liz Smith

Aa.
A for Apple

Aa.
A for Antelope

Aa.
A as in Ant

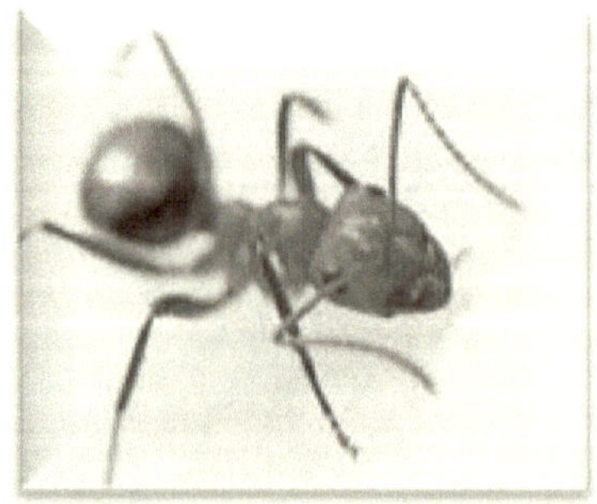

Bb.

B for
Banana

Bb.

B for
Ball

Bb.

B for
Bag

Cc.
C for
Coconut

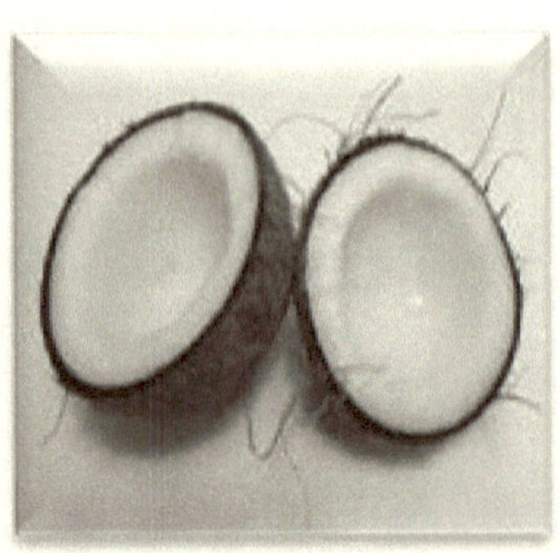

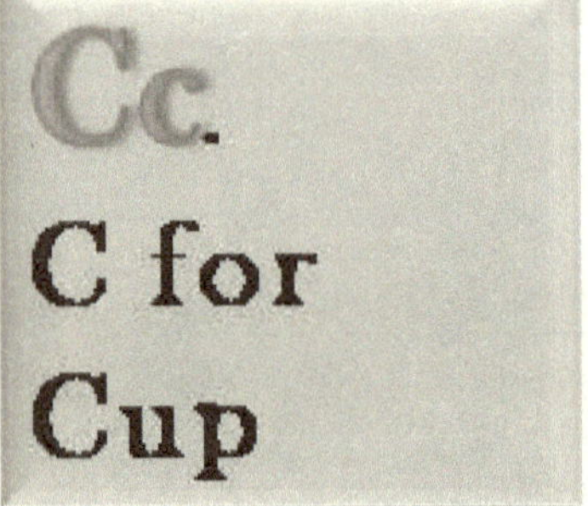
Cc.
C for
Cup

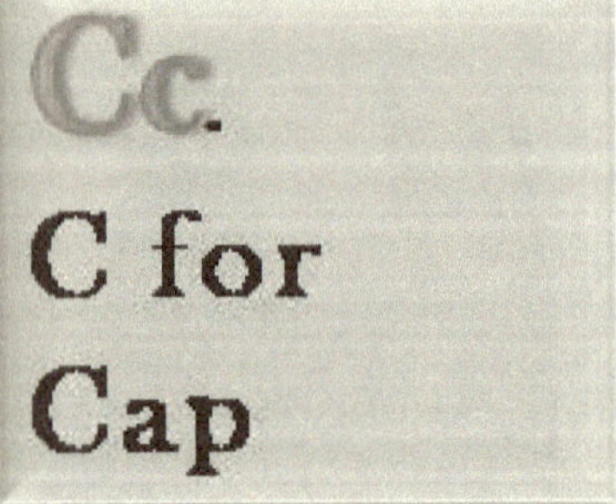
Cc.
C for
Cap

Dd.

D as in Dog

Dd.

D as in Duck

Dd.

D as in Drum

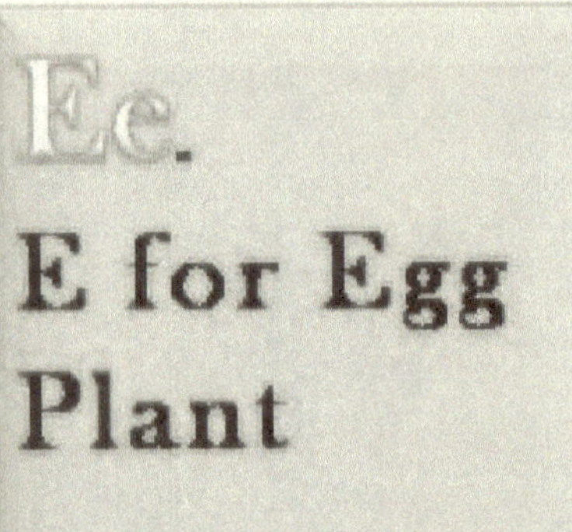

Ee.

E for Egg Plant

Ee.

E for Egg

Ee.

E for Elephant

Ff

F for fruits

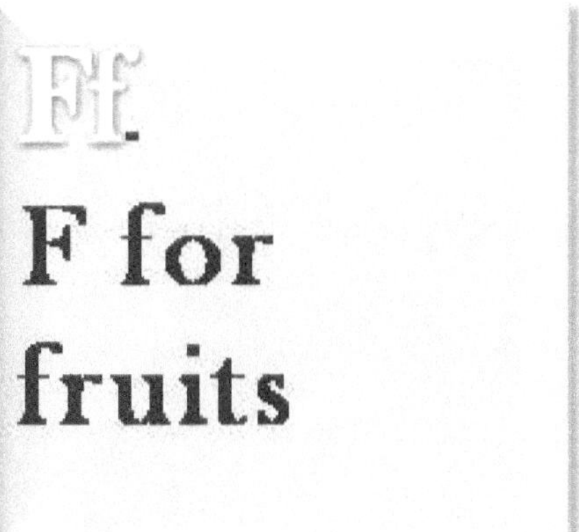

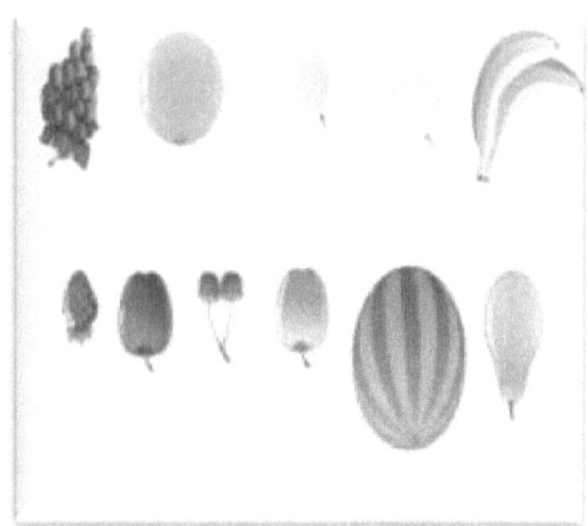

Ff.

F for frog

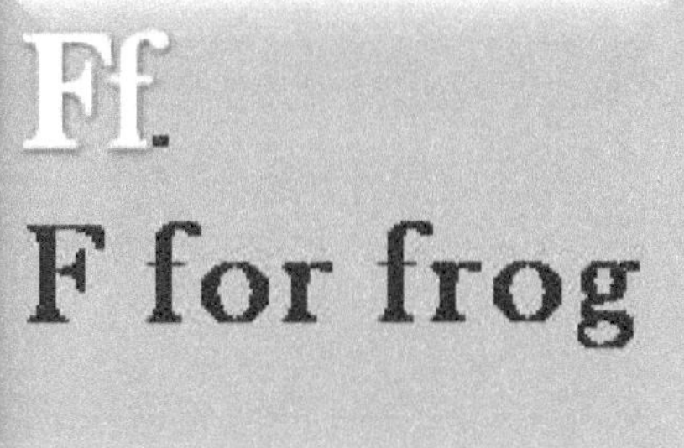

Ff.

F for flower

Gg.
G for Grape

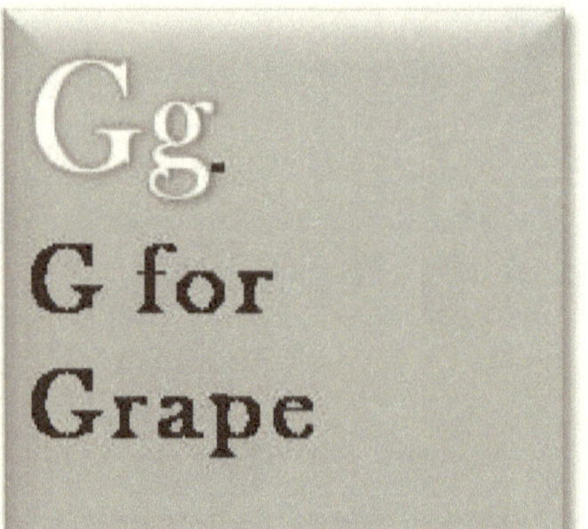

Gg.
G for Goat

Gg.
G for Grasshopper

H.
H as in
Hat

H.
H as in
Hammer

H.
H as in
House

Ii.

I as in Ice Cream

Ii.
I as in
Iron

Ii.
I as in
Ink

Jj.
J as in Jug

Jj.
J as in
Juice

Jj.
J as in
Jam

Kk.

K as in Kettle

K as in Kite

Kk.

K as in King

Ll.
L as in
Lorry

Ll.
L as in
Lion

Ll.
L as in
Lemon

Mm.

M as in Mango

M.
M as in Mat

M.
M as in Moon

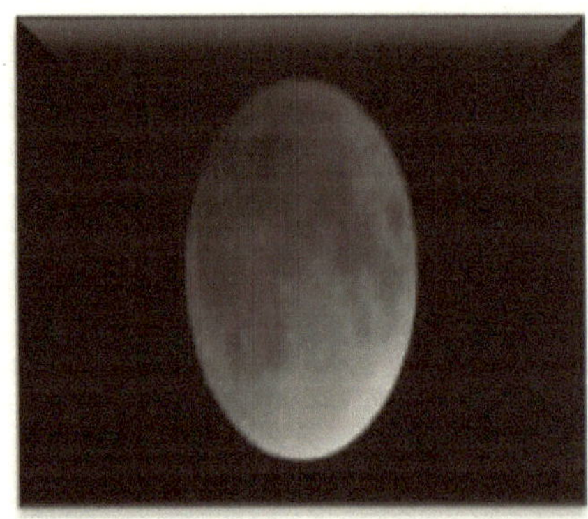

Nn

N as in
Nuts

N.
N as in
Nurse

N.
N as in
Nest

Oo.

O as in Orange

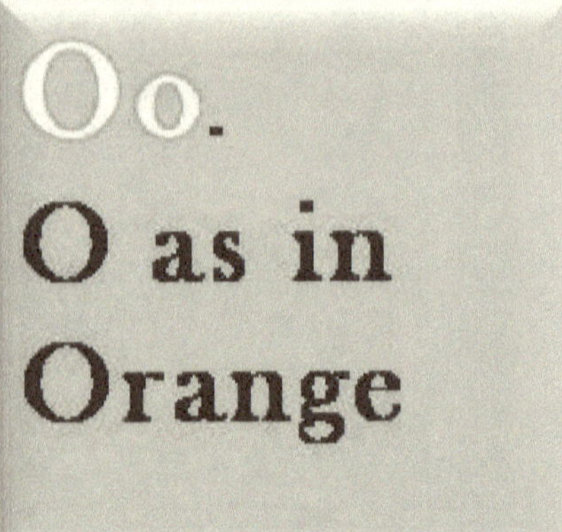

O.
O as in Onions

O.
O as in Owl

Pp.

P as in
Pineapple

P.
P as in
Pencil

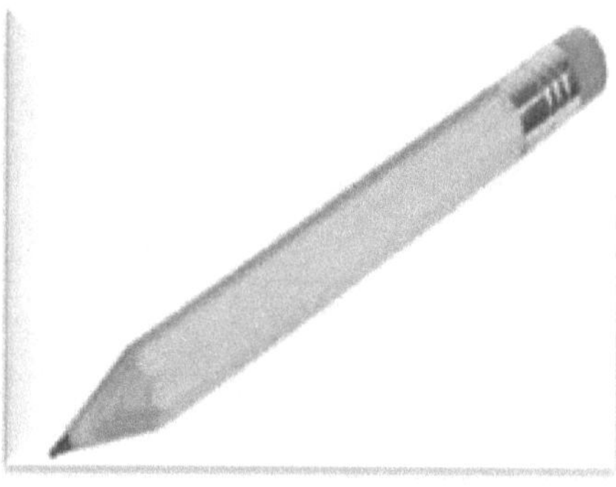

P.
P as in
Pawpaw

Qq.
Q as in
Queen

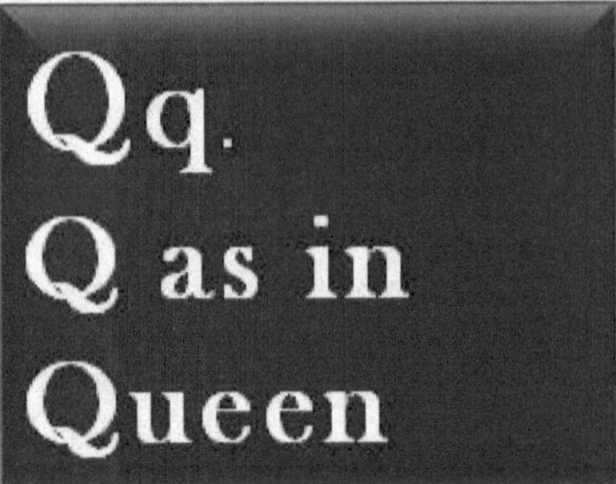

Qq.
Q as in
Quartz

Qq.
Q as in
Quartz

Rr.
R as in
R as in
Raspberry

Rr.
R as in
Rabbit

R.
R as in
Rainbow

Ss.

S as in Sausage

Ss.

S as in Statue

Ss.

S as in Scissors

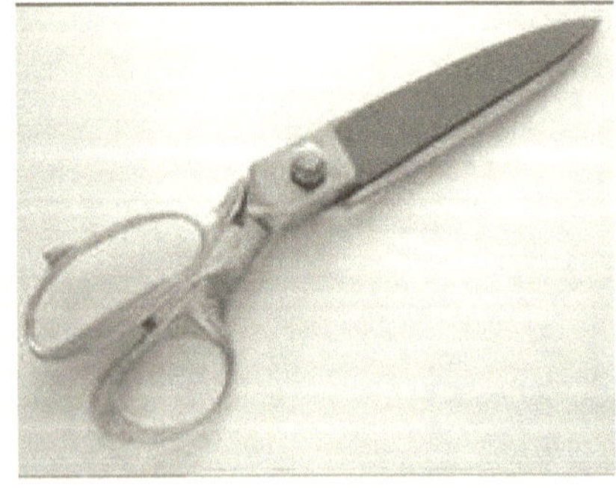

Tt.

T as in
Tomatoes

Tt.

T as in
Table

T.

T as in
Tangerine

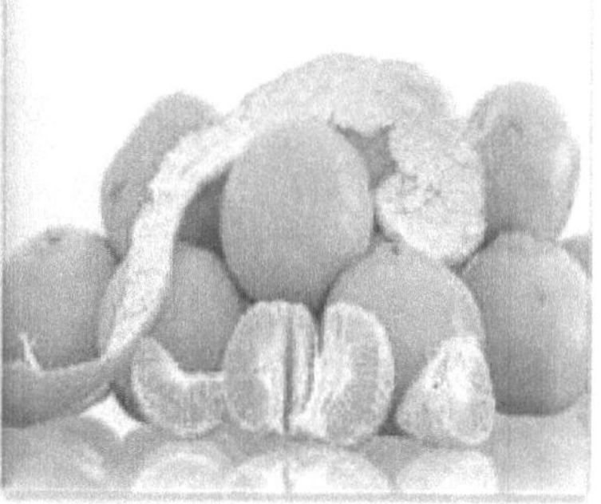

Uu.

U as in Umbrella

Uu

U as in Uniform

Uu.

U as in Unicorn

Vv.
V as in
Vegetables

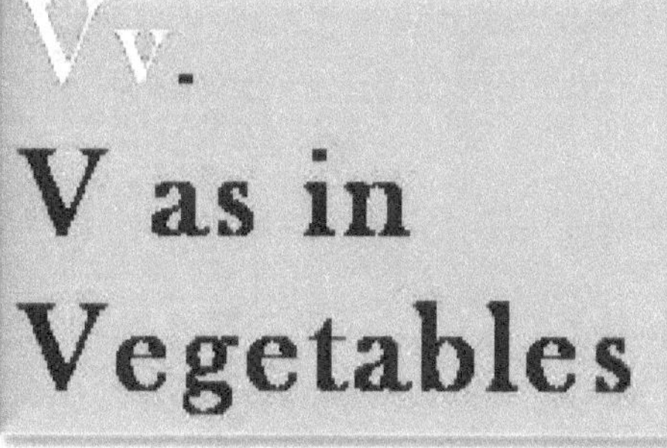

Vv.
V as in
Violin

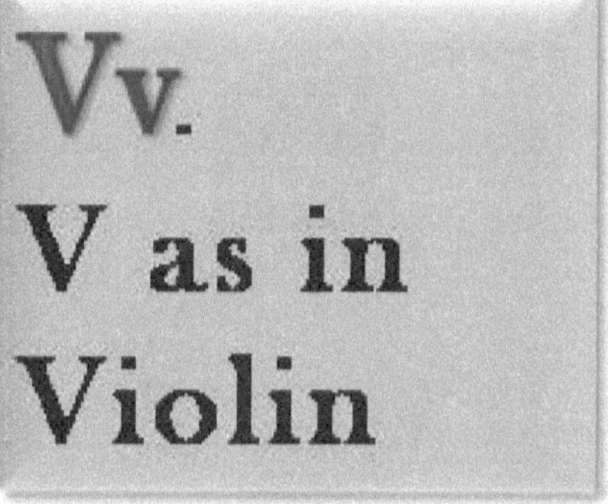

Vv.
V as in
Vegetable Soup

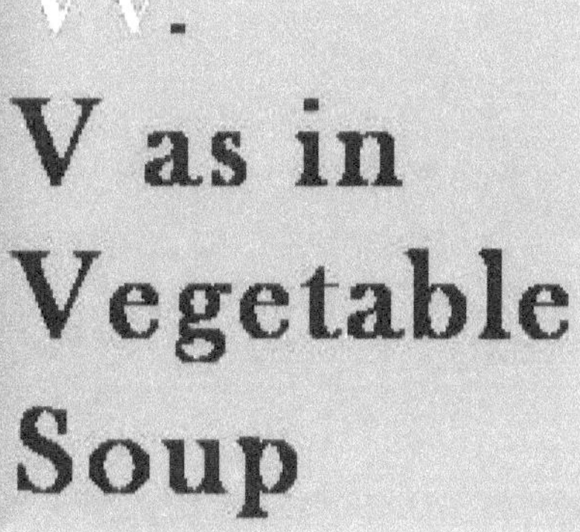

Ww.
W as in water

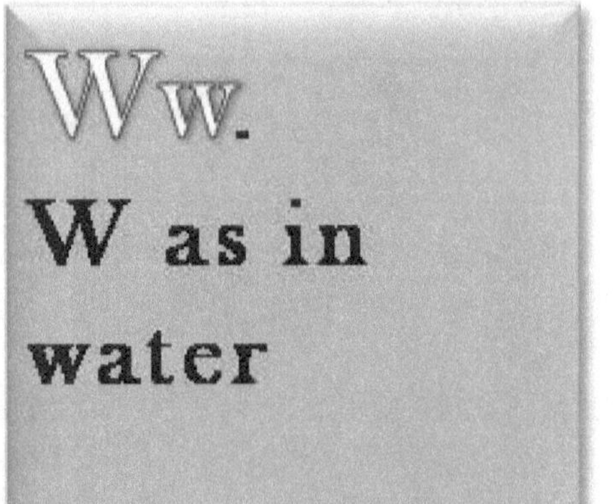

Ww.
W as in watch

Ww.
W as in water melon

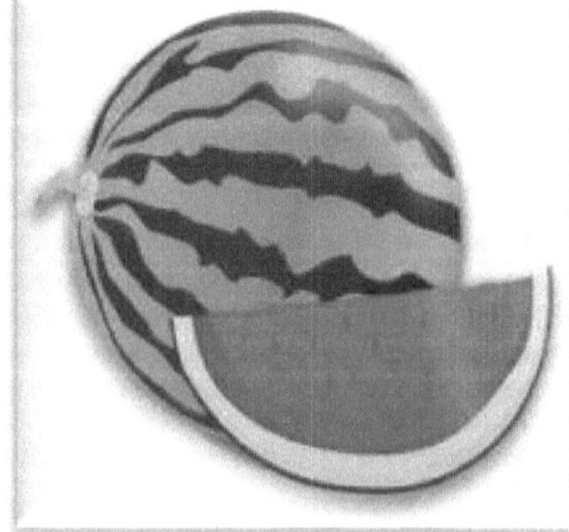

Xx.

X as in Xylophone

Xx.

X as in Xmas Tree

Xx.

X as in X- ray

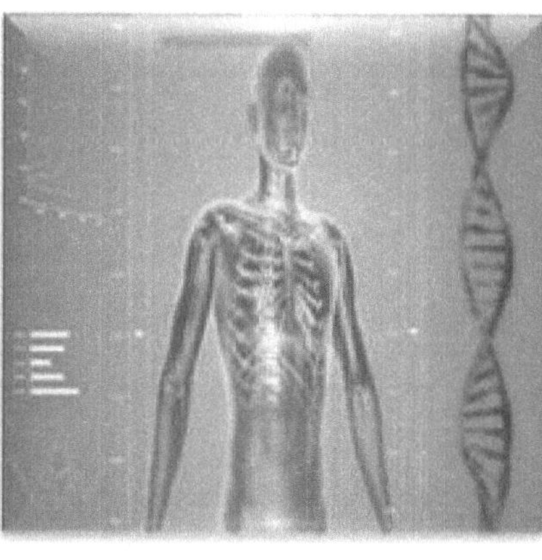

Yy.

Y as in Yam

Yy

Y as in Yolk

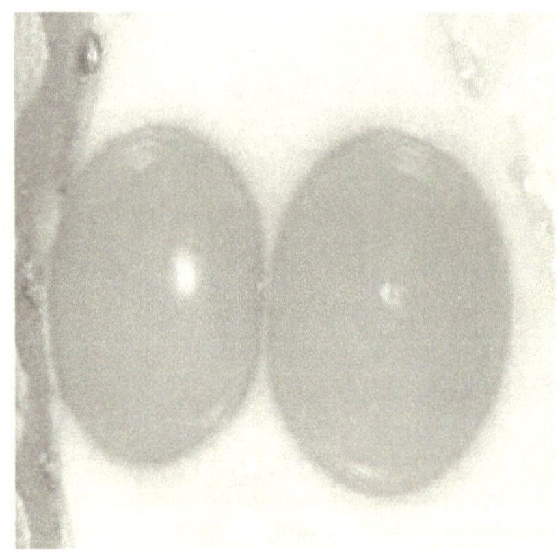

Y.

Y as in Yatch

Zz.

Z as in
Zebra

Zz.

Z as in
Zig -zag

Zz.

Z as in Zip